Life – the love of eternity

eternity – the love of life

Leben – die Liebe der Ewigkeit

Ewigkeit – die Liebe des Lebens

Yale University Press

JOSEF ALBERS   POEMS AND DRAWINGS

Published in North America by
Yale University Press
P.O. Box 209040
New Haven, CT 06520-9040
www.yalebooks.com

First published 1958 by Readymade Press, New Haven, CT

Second edition 1961 published by George Wittenborn, Inc., New York

This third edition published 2006 by order of the Tate Trustees by Tate Publishing,
a division of Tate Enterprises Ltd, Millbank, London SW1P 4RG
www.tate.org.uk/publishing

Library of Congress Cataloging-in-Publication Data
Library of Congress Control Number: 2006921126

ISBN 0-300-12033-8

New material designed by Geoffrey Winston at WinstonWPA
Printed in the UK by TJ International, Padstow

At the end of his life, Josef Albers, by then a legend in the art world and an international success, lived with his wife Anni in a modest raised ranch house on a quiet suburban street in the Connecticut town called Orange. The world-renowned colour theorist marvelled at the sign that marked the town boundary. Painted green, the lettering white, it said, 'This is Orange'; he considered this a perfect example of the trickiness inherent in the names of colours. He was enchanted by the deceptiveness of words and the idea of multiple meanings – visual or verbal.

With that relish of puns and alertness to the vagaries and discrepancies of language, the octogenarian painter, glued, like most of the United States, to the Watergate hearings on television, took particular delight in the idea that one of President Nixon's chief minions, very much embroiled in the corruption, had the name of 'Ehrlichman' – which in German means 'honest man'. Speaking two languages as he did, Albers was sharply aware of what a twist of the truth that name communicated.

The interplay of German and English caught his fancy; so did the balance of simplicity and complexity as one latched on to apprehensible details in a fluctuating world, opting for what was dependable – like the shapes of squares – as a stronghold amidst the infinite and

mysterious universe of colour, using few words and short lines as a handle to the vast worlds of form and language.

In that plain clapboard house on Birchwood Drive, Albers's bedroom looked like a modern version of a medieval monk's cell. There was nothing whatsoever on the walls, which were made of cold drywall painted a flat white. The garage was full of the artist's colourful *Homages to the Square*, lined up like matching books on a shelf, but their creator chose to look at none of them in the room where he read and slept. His bed was a plain mattress on a base with short wooden legs: nothing more. The desk, which he had made at Black Mountain College, consisted of two wooden planks, accompanied by a standard kitchen chair. The bookshelves and cupboards were procured from a store for office equipment; they were intended for a bank or an accountant's office, not for domestic living.

But in that room, at his bedside, Josef Albers always had a rather splendid looking leather-bound edition of nineteenth-century German Romantic poetry. This was how he chose to lose himself every evening – in the verse he had known since childhood.

Poetry was an essential part of Albers's life. He liked Schiller and Goethe; he also liked Haiku. And he was immensely proud of his own forays in the field – especially of the work that had been first published in

Poems and Drawings in 1958. This book contained a great deal of what the artist cherished: quietude and a look of modesty, the mix of the visual and the verbal. It put mysterious drawings, utterly lean and simple but with multiple meanings, against verse with the same qualities. Through this particular combination of elements, he had made something musical: where the phrasing and the voids count as much as the central themes, where weight is dissipated and rhythm constant.

The drawings in *Poems and Drawings* belong to a type Albers called 'Structural Constellations'. They demonstrate in an utterly refined and straightforward way his notion of 'the discrepancy between physical fact and psychic effect', and his belief that, while in mathematics and science the sum of one plus one is two, in art one plus one can equal three or more. If a viewer takes the requisite time with these drawings, they offer multiple and contradictory meanings; they invite you to read a space as being at first glance like a box viewed from the outside and on a second look like a container open at the end; they make straight lines appear curved or bent, they make parallel lines seem angled in relation to one another, they make flat trapezoidal planes twist like bent metal. The poetry, too, while deceptively simple and easy to read, invites endless reflection, suggesting, invariably, far more

readings than appear to be offered at first.

Poems and Drawings was also significant for Albers as a perfect object. He was obsessed with graphic layout, had written passionately on the subject, and cared intensely about both aesthetics and legibility. I had known of his concern with the printer's and graphic designer's craft ever since I had first met him. I well remember the occasion of my initiation; I was a graduate student in art history at Yale University, where he had headed the Department of Design fifteen years earlier and which was in New Haven, about fifteen minutes away from the house in Orange. I had been brought to the ranch house by an older friend who collected Albers's work. The great Bauhausler had greeted me by asking, 'What do you do, boy?'

'I'm studying Art History at Yale, Sir,' I replied.

'Do you like it, boy?'

I was nervous that truthfulness might cost me my fellowship funds, but the boldness of the great man with his shock of smooth white hair made it impossible for me to dissemble. 'No, Sir, not really.'

'Why not, boy?'

I explained that I was losing my passion for looking at art, my ability to feel the beauty and grace of the work, and was feeling encumbered with facts. After I gave an example of the detailed research I was assigned to do,

he asked, 'Which of those bastards in art history don't
you like?'

My answer pleased him, and then he asked, 'What
does your father do?' Of my two parents, my mother,
a painter with a studio in the house, was the more
excited that I was going to be meeting Josef Albers that
day, but he seemed to care more about the male parent,
so I answered that my father was a printer, that he
owned a company that mainly did commercial offset
work. 'Good, boy, then you're not just an art historian;
then you know something about something,' Albers
replied with a grin.

This became his reason for talking to me a great
deal about printing. He had worked with some fine
lithographers, and was fascinated by their technique.
He had only recently met a screenprinter who managed
to make *Homages to the Square* with such tight
registration between colours that there was no need for
one colour to be superimposed on another; rather, each
could be printed on pure white paper, with no overlap
of the hues and a perfect tight fit. Little in life thrilled
him as much as technical mastery and refinement.

He was also deeply involved with typefaces. Albers
began to give me his books of type, and to point out
the ones he most liked. Bodoni and Garamond were
often his choices for his own publications, and he had
a passion for Sabon. Serif types, he believed, were always
better for text. He explained to me that the serif had
been developed by people inscribing gravestones
because, when they ended the stroke of the chisel, they
invariably left a light mark; the inadvertent result of
that mechanical necessity was the discovery that the
serif served to carry the eye from letter to letter and
facilitate reading. Serifs, like adequate margins, made
a printed page work better.

On one of my visits to the house on Birchwood
Drive – I had begun to go there regularly after the
first grilling interview – Albers gave me, as a present,
Poems and Drawings, explaining that this small volume,
designed by his friend and colleague Norman Ives,
exemplified his points.

Ives was both a screenprinter and a graphic designer.
Additionally, with his business partner Sewell Sillman,
he installed Albers's exhibitions – at the Sidney Janis
Gallery in New York, at least every two years, and, in
1971, at the Metropolitan Museum of Art, where Albers
was the first living artist in America honoured by a
solo show. Ives understood the balance of white space
needed to surround Albers's paintings as well as his words
and his drawings. That relationship of artist and designer
was one of the most important in Josef Albers's life, and
Poems and Drawings one of its finest by-products.

The first edition of *Poems and Drawings* was
published by Readymade Press in 1958 in an edition
of 500 copies. A small publishing operation, Readymade
Press operated in the printing offices of Yale University
Press in a basement on York Street in New Haven. This
was during Albers's time at Yale, and he had a storage
room in the same basement. The location made it easy
for him to look at proofs or even watch press work as
he walked in or out of the space where he kept
everything from glass constructions he had made at the
Bauhaus to current magazines featuring him and his
work. Norman Ives was also living near New Haven,
and was regularly in and out of that print shop. Thus
it was possible to facilitate this work according to the
meticulous standards of these two people who were
obsessed with quality, determined for perfectly neat
impressions and resolved to achieve just the right tone
of the black ink.

A decade later, George Wittenborn, owner of the
legendary bookstore at 1018 Madison Avenue (then
the best place in America to buy art books) made a
second edition. There were a few variations from the
first edition: the word 'Weg', for example, having been
translated as 'road' the first time became 'path' in the
second version. Beyond these refinements, comparable
to the changing of a colour in an *Homage to the Square*,
the verbal equivalent of switching a Grumbacher
Mars Yellow with a Winsor & Newton Mars Yellow,
the editions were the same.

Albers always hoped for a third edition. He had kept
a list of the names of everyone who could be identified
who had bought copies during the book's first lifetime
(Readymade Press sold directly to individuals, rather
than through bookstores, so this could be charted) and
was especially pleased by the libraries and institutions
that owned copies. In 1973, when the artist was
eighty-five years old, George Wittenborn proposed an
updated version to Yale University Press, but nothing
came of the idea. There is no doubt that the artist
would have been absolutely delighted by the decision
of Tate Publishing to take on the project, and by the
very Albersian care with which they have done so.

Nicholas Fox Weber
February 2006

This new publication also provides the occasion to make public for the first time some poems by Josef Albers that until now have been unpublished. These delicate stanzas have, in fact, been almost completely unknown, because they stem from a very private episode of the artist's life.

In the late 1940s, Josef and Anni Albers took a sabbatical in New Mexico. Unknown to Anni, Josef was involved with the landlady of the adobe guesthouse where they were staying. (One assumes, anyway, that this was unknown to Anni. Sometimes Josef's dalliances occurred with her awareness; there was at least one occasion of his discussing one of his affairs with her, and asking her to help him break it off.) Josef wrote some poems for the woman, Betty Seymour, who, a few years following Josef's death, gave them to this author.

As does most of his poetry, the lines of verse to the beguiling woman in New Mexico show the playful and tender side of Josef Albers – and his mischievous streak. They exhibit the fancifulness as well as the ardour that lie beneath the cool veneer of his art of the period.

One does not know the desert

nor its embracing sky

from having seen it only once

One little walk through the night

does not show all of its magic

Two tiny sips won't satisfy

but heighten only thirst

Three meals a day can feed the body

but not two hungry eyes

Dimmed light may emphasize a contour

and candlelight the face

But to know and to do something well —

one needs time and more time again

and plenty of full light

C'razus

I can't lie down

without calling

again and again

a name

and over and over

again

If people could hear me

they would call me crazy

but I would not

mind it

because because

I am

I can't close my eye

without seeing

somebody

I saw only once

in too late

a light

But the moon

is increasing

and soon

will be full

C'razus

Bettselchen

we feel lonesome

but have lighted

a candle

in a ruby-red glass

for somebody

whom we love

to have with us

and whom

we are missing.

love, Jofez

The last month of last year

was not a twelfth one;

still the desert is red

and the Christmas candle

still glowing

Last year's last day

did neither reach the hour twelve

when fading in the dark;

like a walk which came

to no end

That year, as the month

and the day, cannot be over:

I am still walking and

living on it

for Anni

Meine Erde

dient auch andern

meine Welt

gehört nur mir

My earth

serves also others

my world

is mine alone

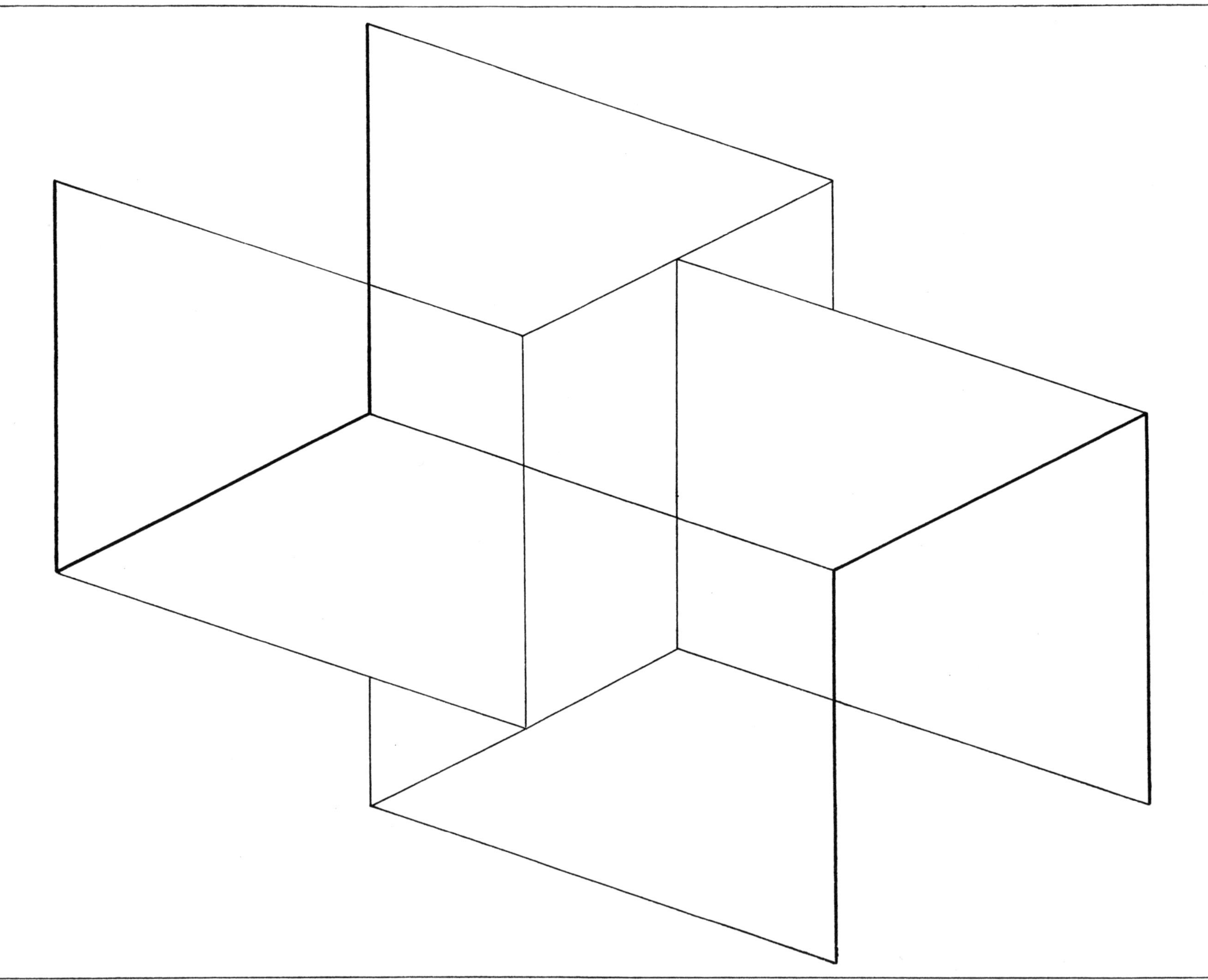

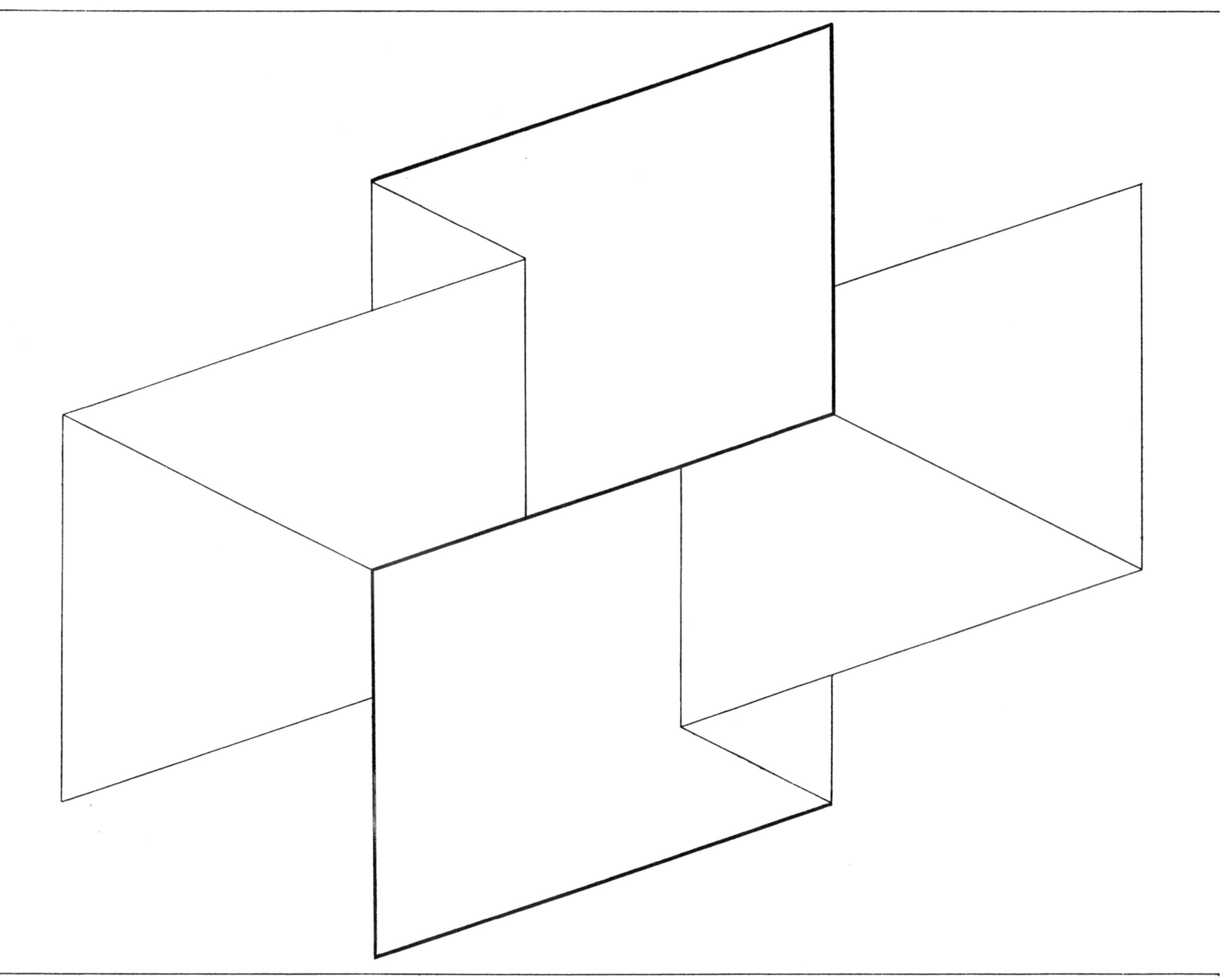

Wenn ich an Dich denke

fällt mir oft was ein

Wozu sind die Blaubeer'n rot

und die schwarzen abgegessen

und der einzig reife Apfel

grad vom Auto überfahren

wenn ich wandre will es regnen

oder jemand mit mir sprechen

dazu geht die Farbe aus

eh' das Bild ist fertig

ach, wonach soll ich nun trachten

da ich so nicht sollte sein

When thinking of you

it enters my head

why now are the blueberries red

and the black ones all eaten

and the only ripened apple

just run over by a car

when I want to walk it starts to rain

or someone comes to see me

besides all this the paint gave out

before the picture was finished

what now shall I aspire to

for so I was not meant to be

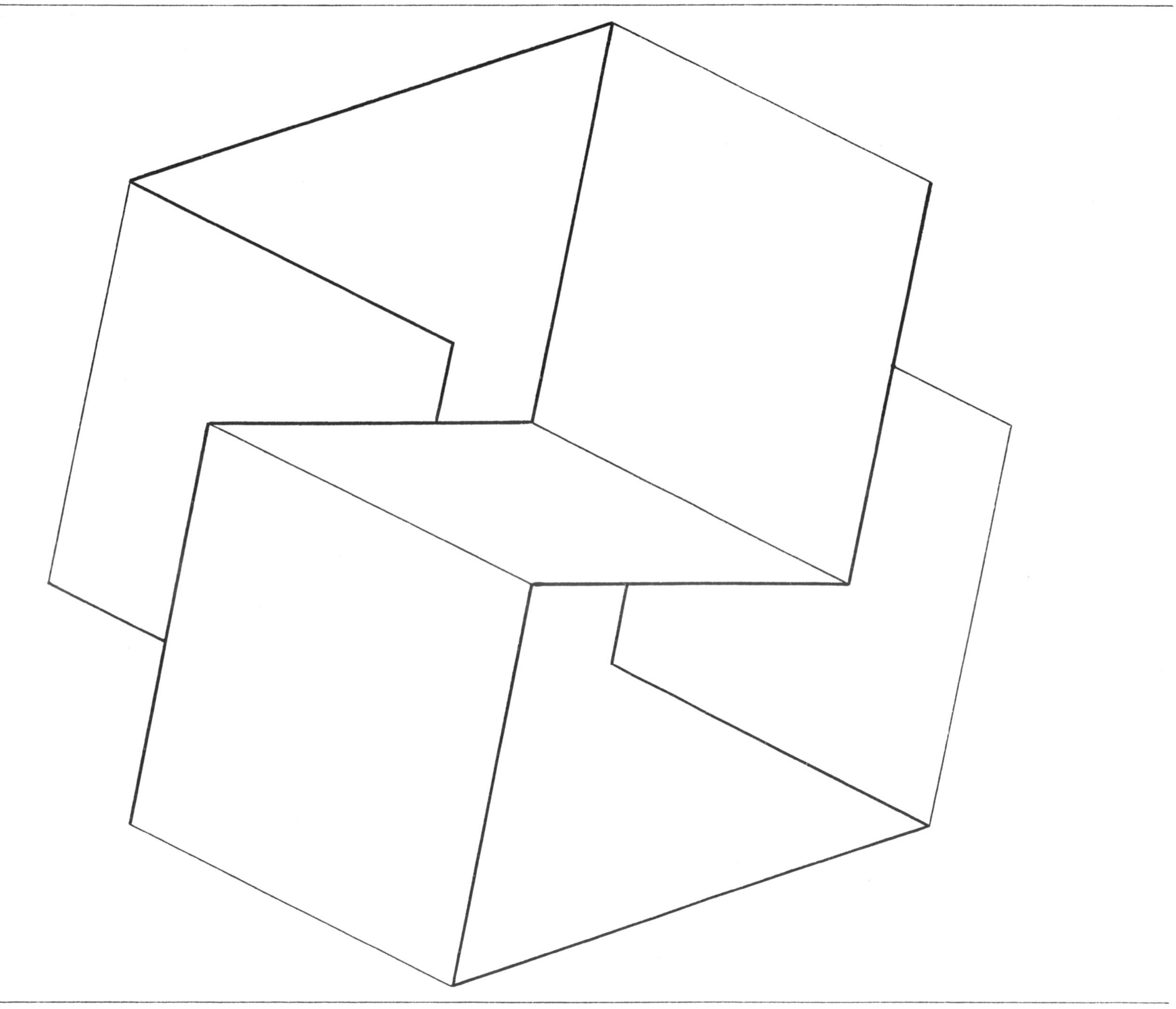

The aim of life

is living creatures

The aim of art

is living creations

Das Ziel des Lebens :

lebende Wesen

Das Ziel der Kunst :

lebende Werke

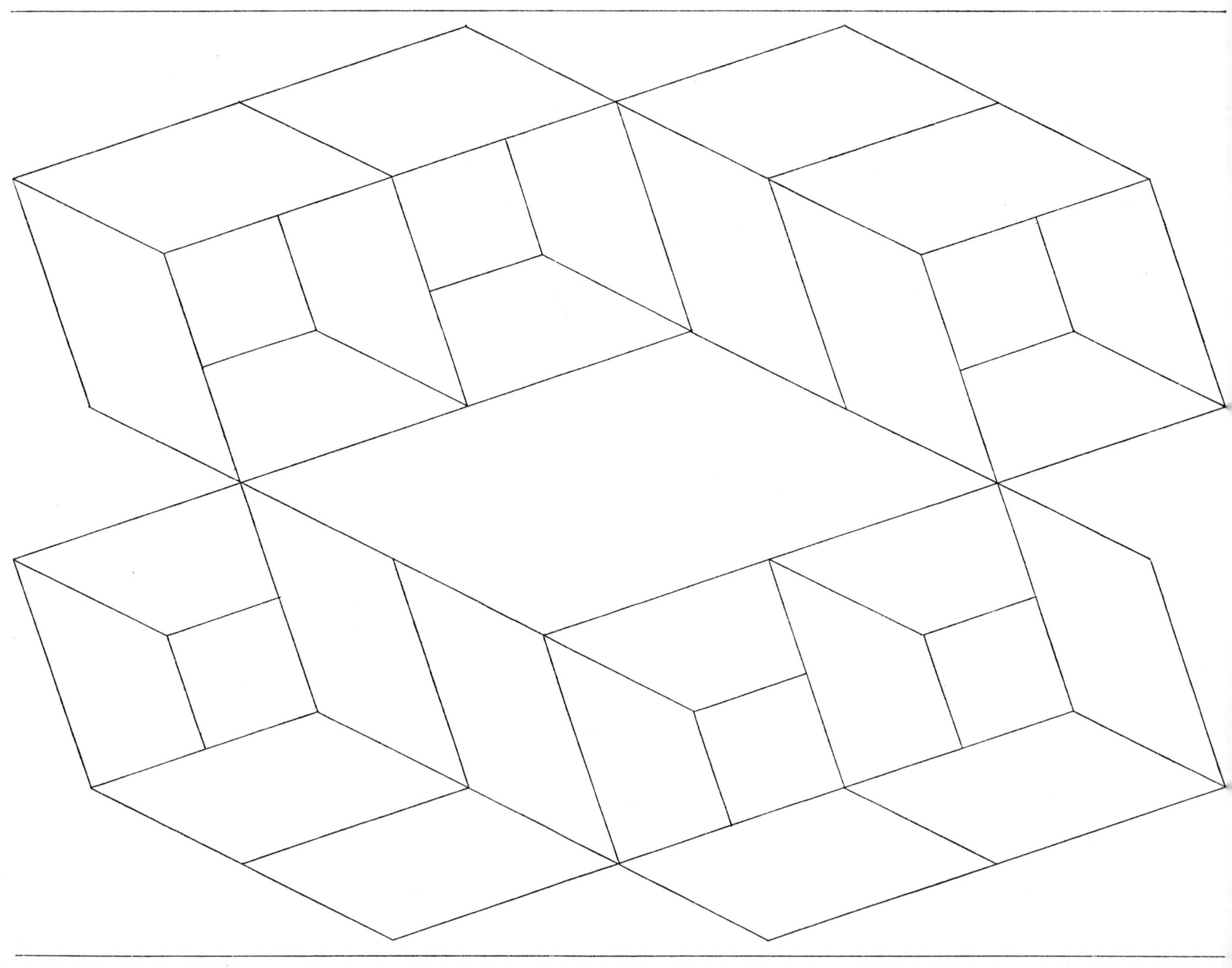

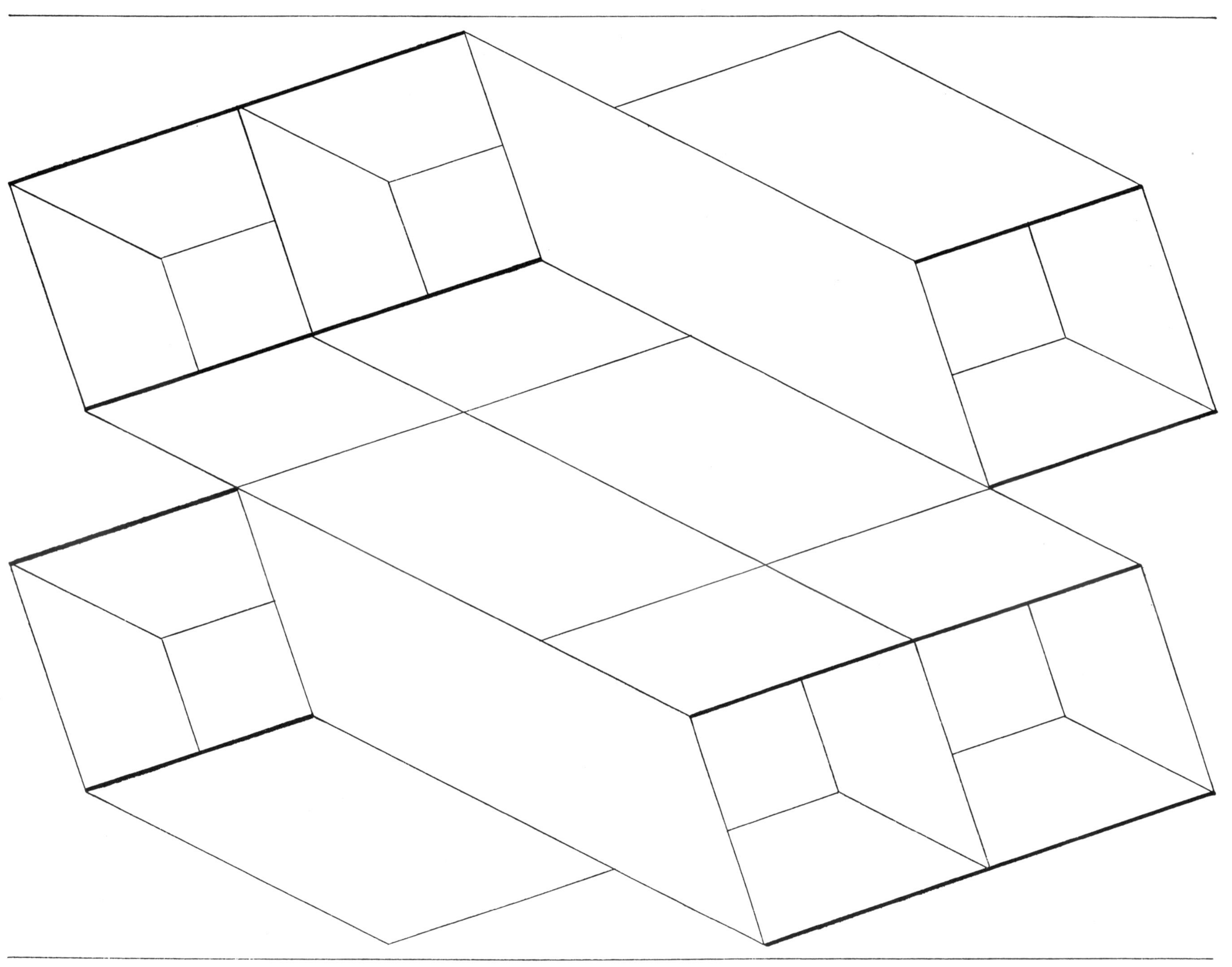

This is a summer noon

on Sunday

when all of nature feels

it's done a week of work

that there is rest and calm

before another working

starts

Like us the air is sweetly

tired

is praying over grass

and flowers

up to the milky blue

The trees are softly breathing

amazed that none of us

went by

The brook sounds horizontal

lines

and cardinals add beads to them

all red and pink and orange

Dies ist ein Sonntag

Sommermittag

Wenn überall Natur uns sagt

dass einer Woche Werk getan

und nun die Zeit für Ruh

bevor ein neues Schaffen folgt

Die Luft gleich uns

ist süss ermüdet

schwebt betend über Gras

und Blumen

bis hoch ins weiche Blau

Die Bäume atmen sanft

und sind erstaunt

dass niemand kommt vorbei

Der Bach summt vor sich

flache Linien

und Vögel fügen Perlen bei

gold rosa all und gelb

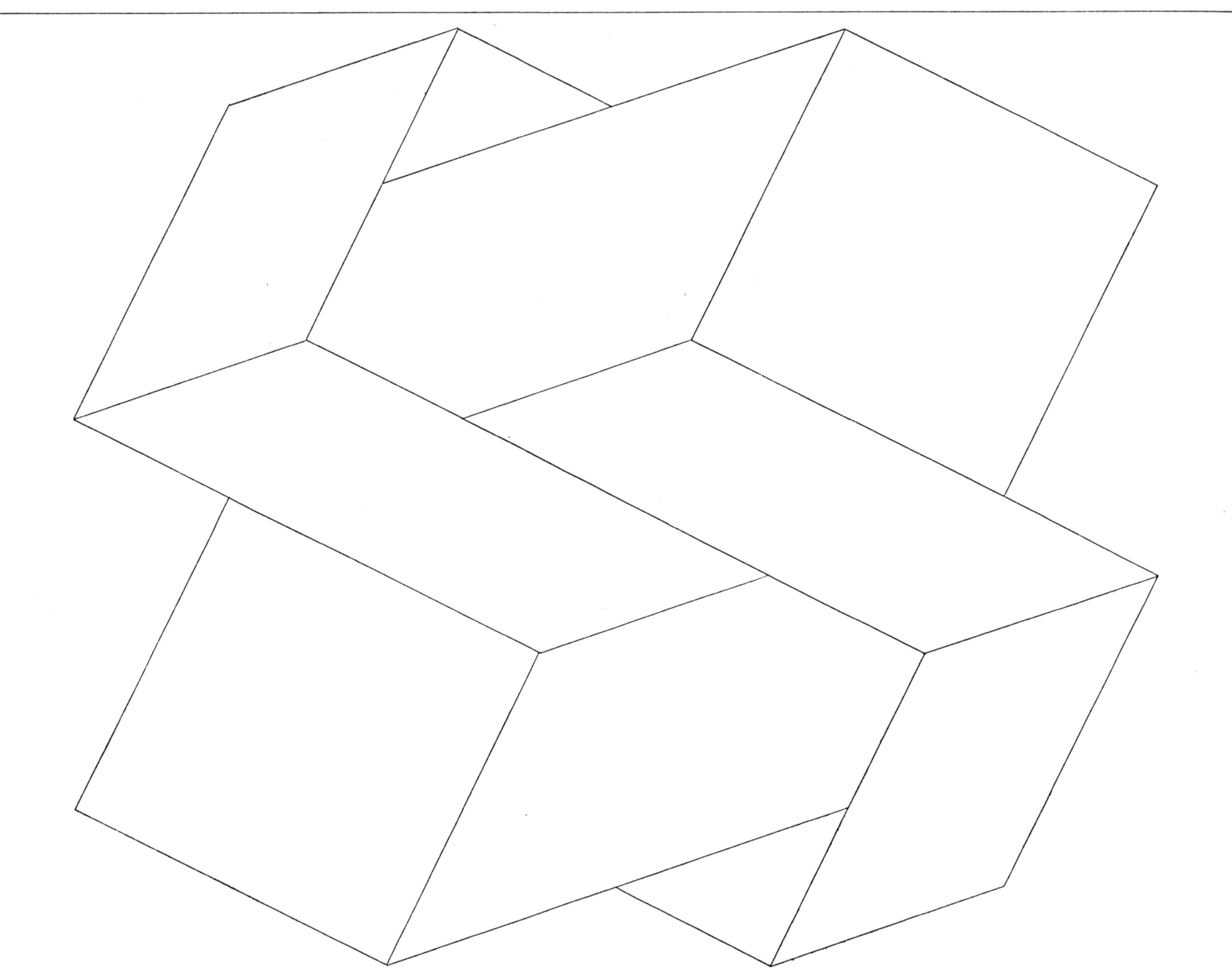

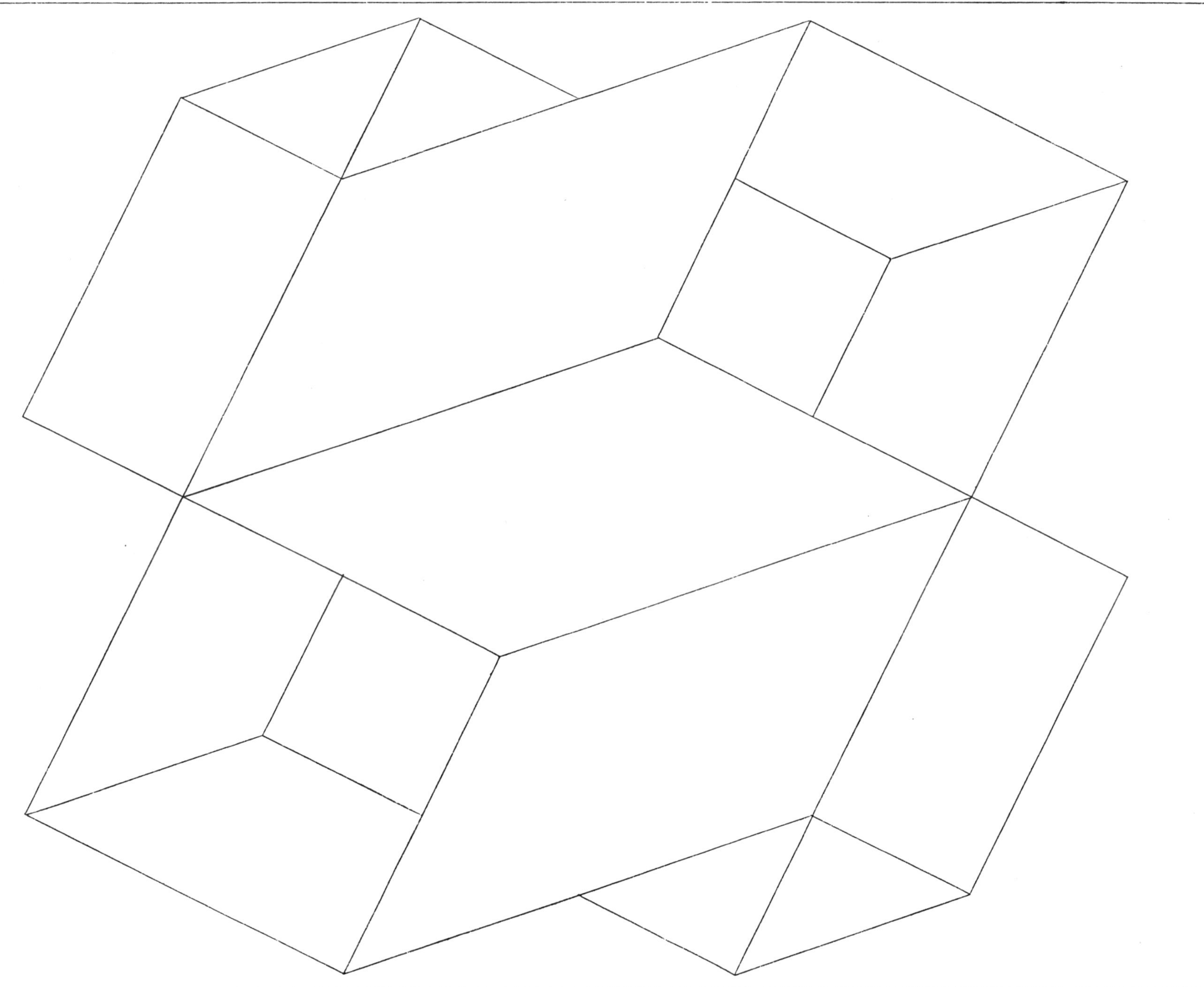

Einer geht

einer steht

wer hat mehr recht

auf den Weg

One is walking

one is standing

who is more entitled

to the path

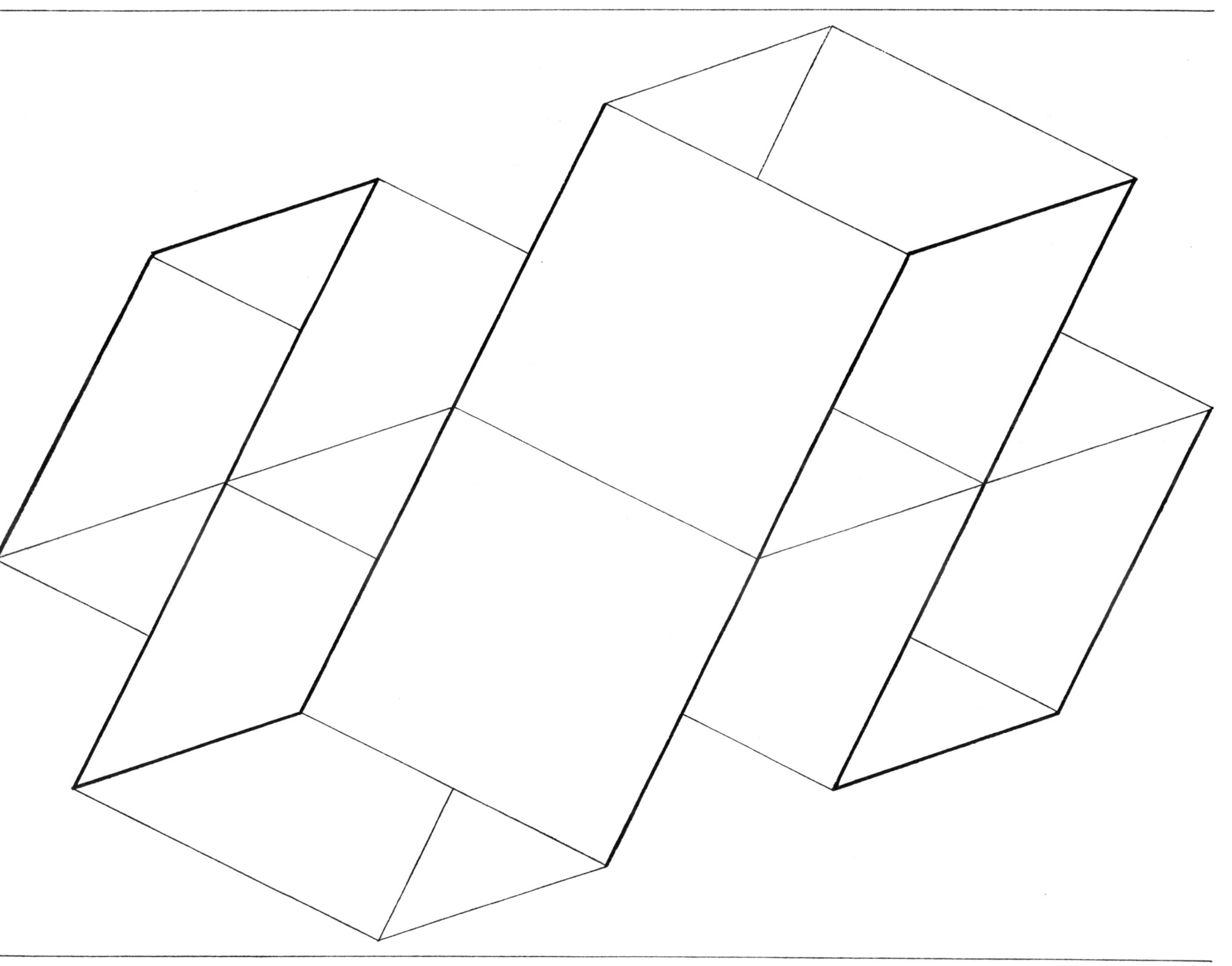

Ich habe eine Blume

in der Hand

und weiss nicht

was zu tun

Soll ich sie

sehen nur

und halten

oder hüten

Sie ist doch

eine Blume

und ich bin

doch nur ich

Verzeihe Gott

dass ich sie pflückte

I am holding a flower

in my hand

and know not

what to do

Should I but see

this flower

or keep it

cherish it

It is a flower

and I am only I

Forgive me God

for taking it

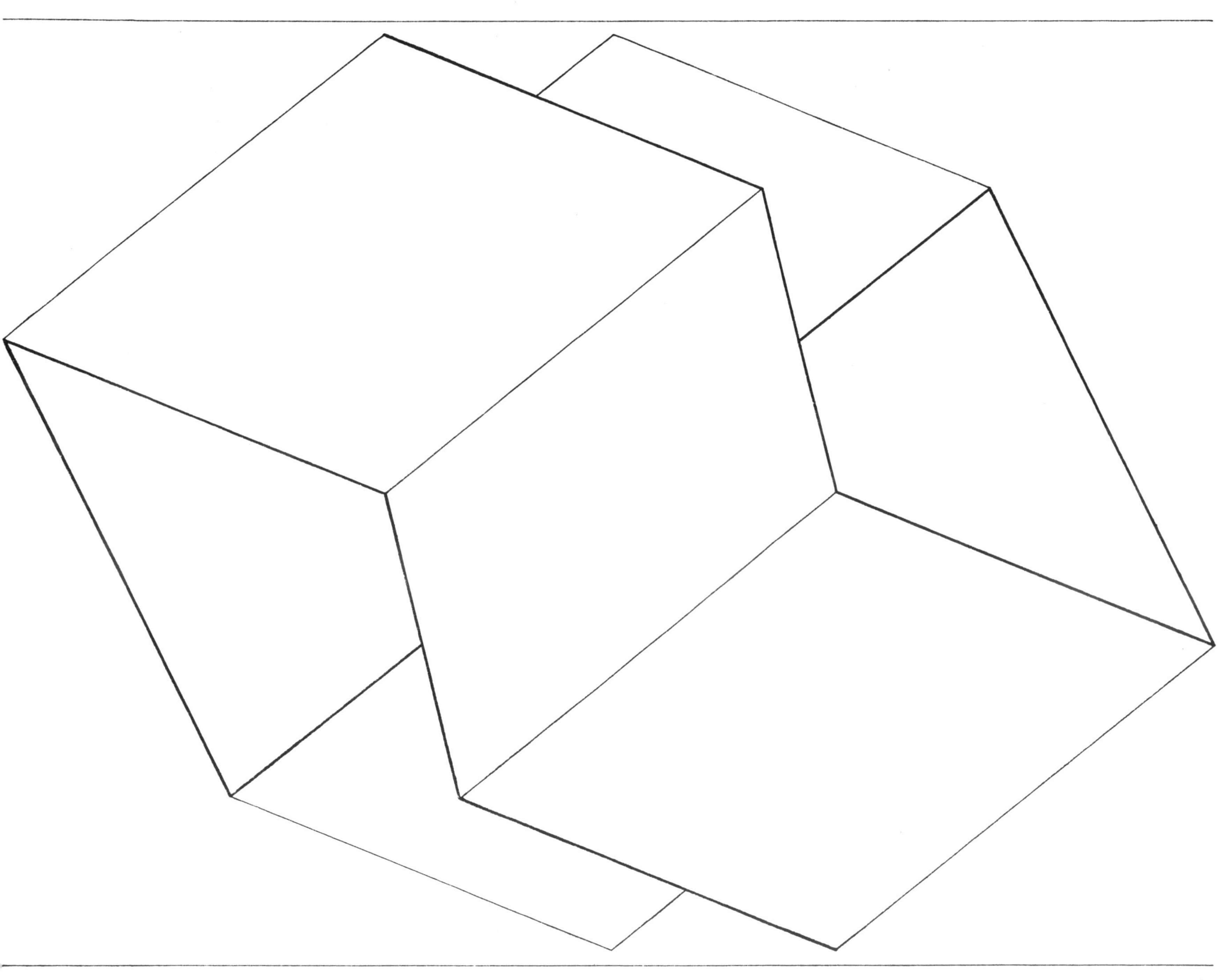

PLATON II *(An einen Dialektiker)*

Weise sein, ein grosser Wunsch

weise scheinen, breiter Brauch

Weiser hört mehr als man sagte

weiss und sagt mehr als er redet

halbe Einsicht macht viel sprechen

aber Wörter sind nicht Worte

Denken lebt selbst in der Wüste

wirkt auch ohne Mund und Hörer

Leonardo folgte eignem Denken

wollte nicht Apelles sein

Weisheit trachtet nicht nach Pulten

Grösse steht in eignem Werke

also : Platon ist nur einmal

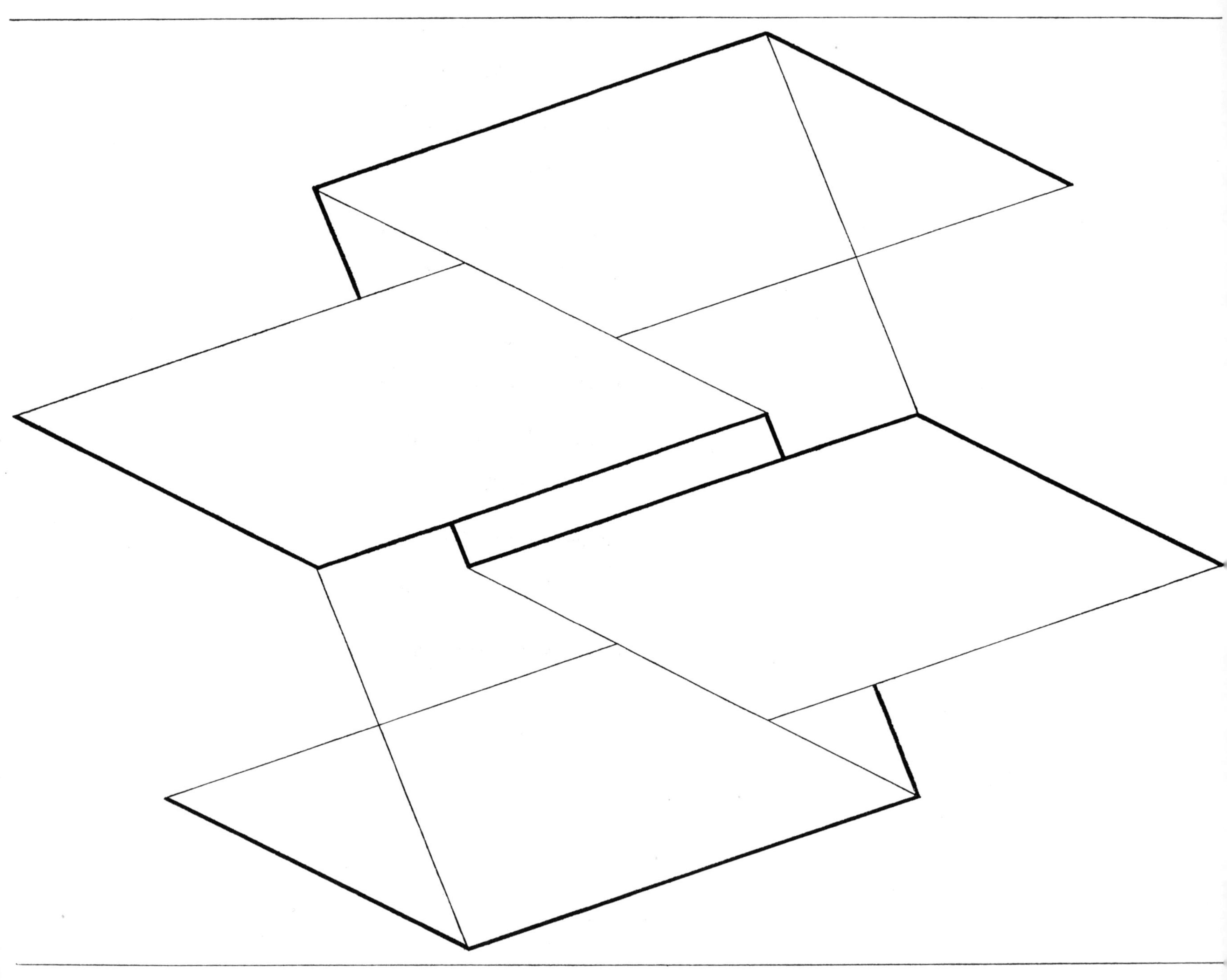

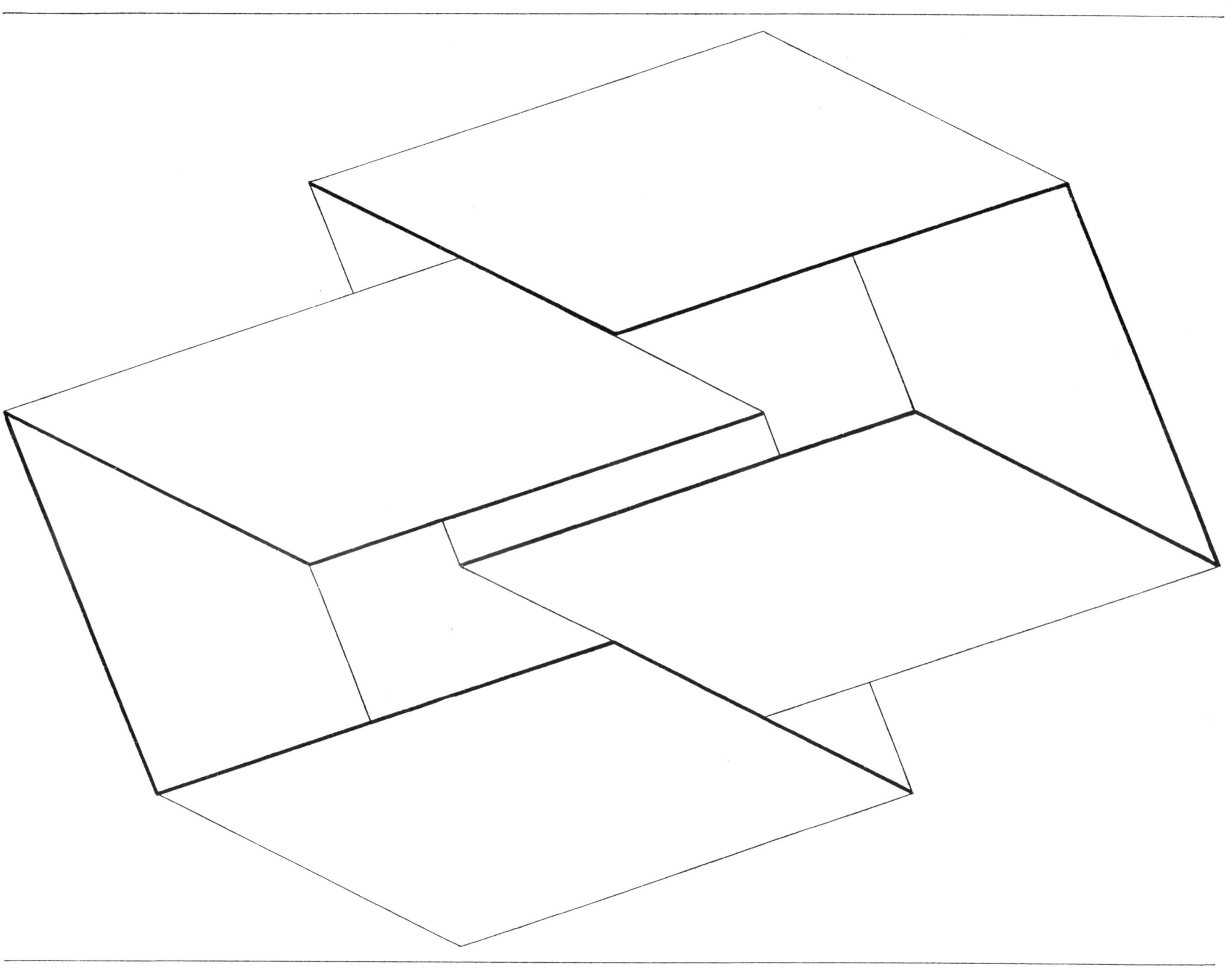

Wenn Rhododendron blumen

und Feuerfliegen leuchten

Wenn Sonne, Luft, und Schwimmen

dann sind die Ferien

Dann glauben wir an freie Zeit

für ruhen, sinnen, sammeln

vor leerem Schreibpapier

und weisser Leinewand

When rhododendrons bloom

and fireflies light up

when there is sun and air and swimming

then there are holidays

then we believe in having time

to rest, to think, to gather our thoughts

before blank paper

and an empty canvas

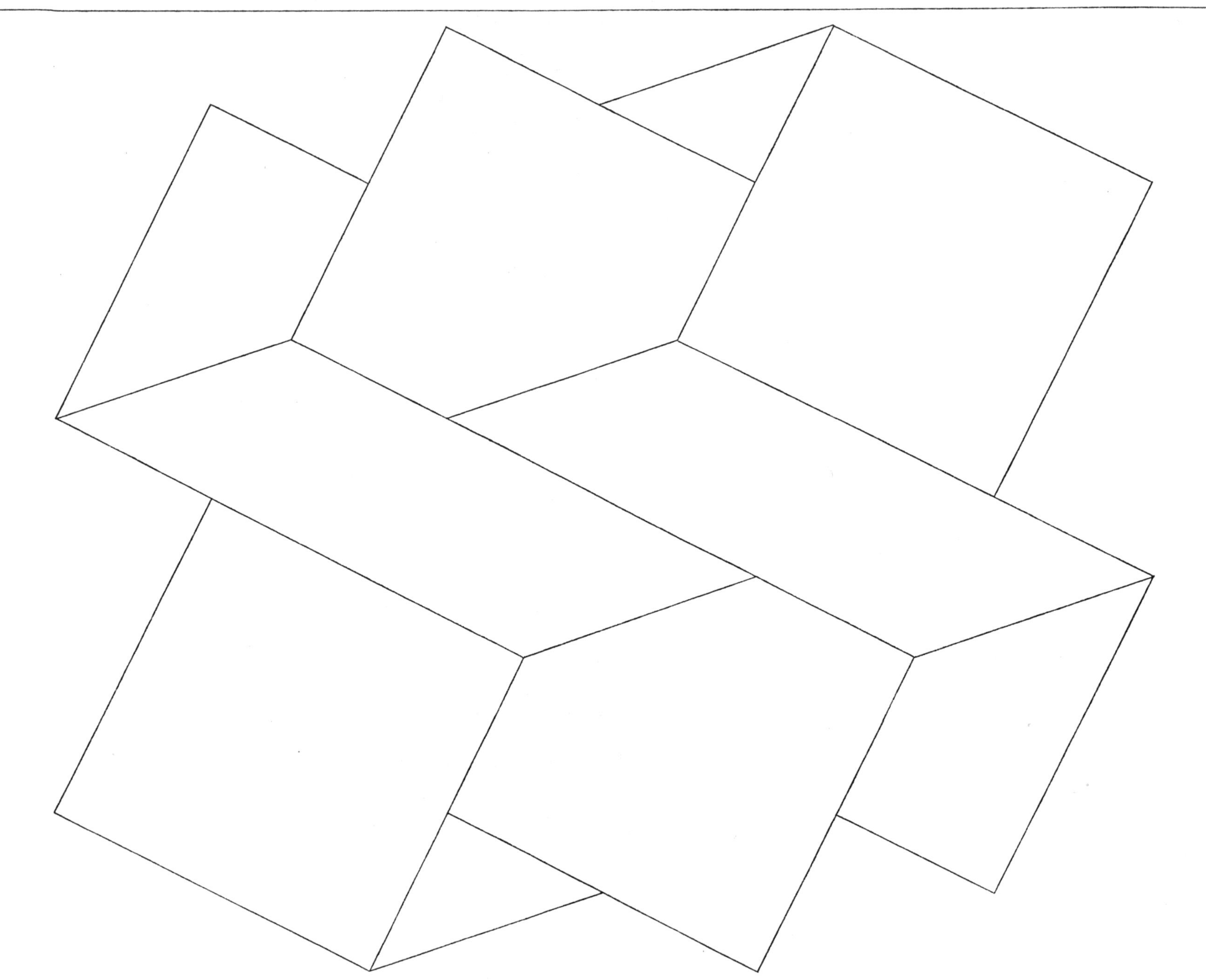

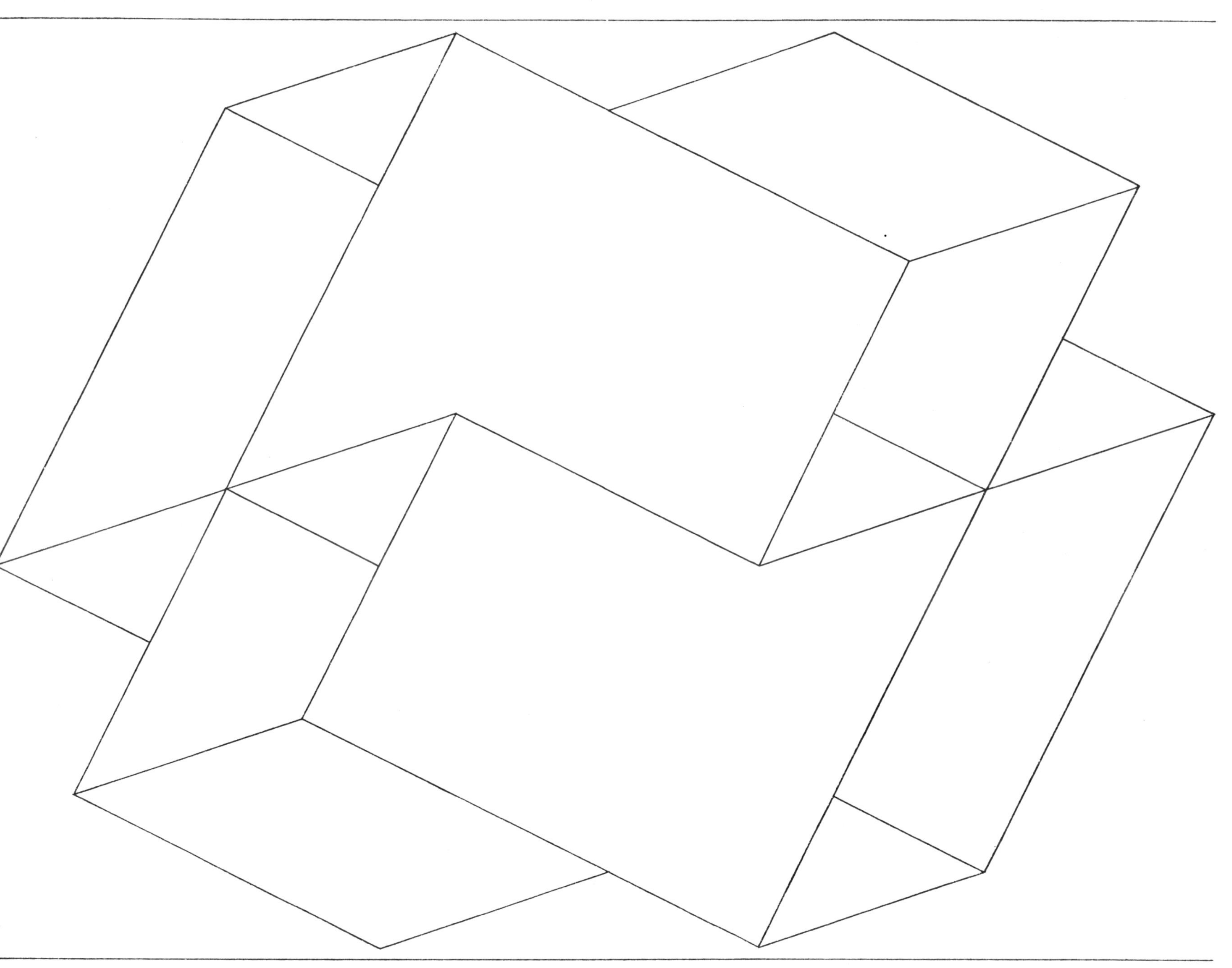

MEHR ODER WENIGER

Leicht – zu wissen

dass Brillanten – teuer

gut – zu lernen

dass Rubine – tiefer

mehr – zu sehen

dass auch Kiesel – Wunder sind

MORE OR LESS

Easy – to know

that diamonds – are precious

good – to learn

that rubies – have depth

but more – to see

that pebbles – are miraculous

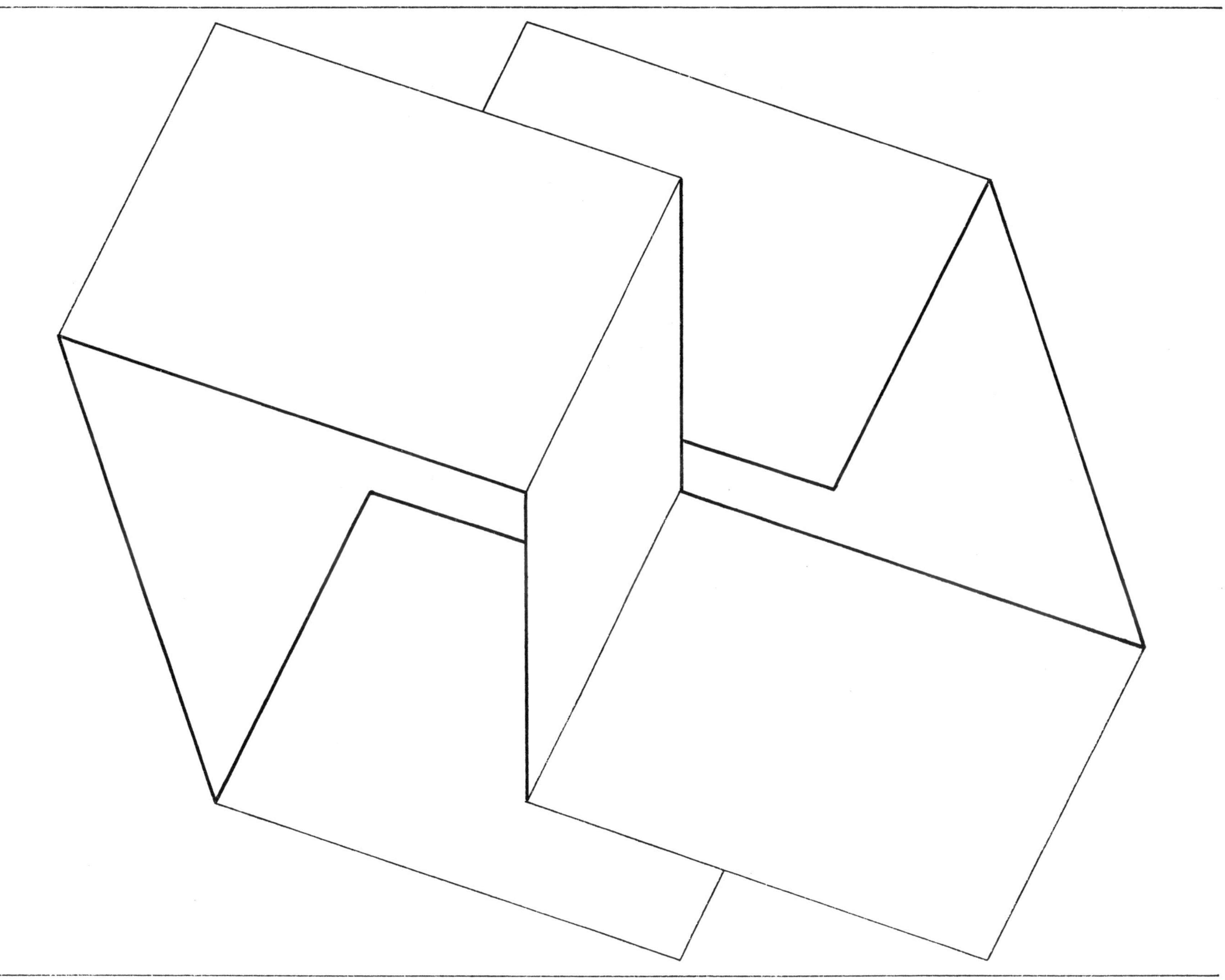

WERTHERISCH

Wenn die Luft

getönt mit Blumen

duftend Vogelsang

dann muss ich zurück

mich sehnen

weiss nur nicht – wohin

IN THE MANNER OF WERTHER

When the days are

tinted with flowers

and scented with song

then I am longing

to return

but wonder – where to go

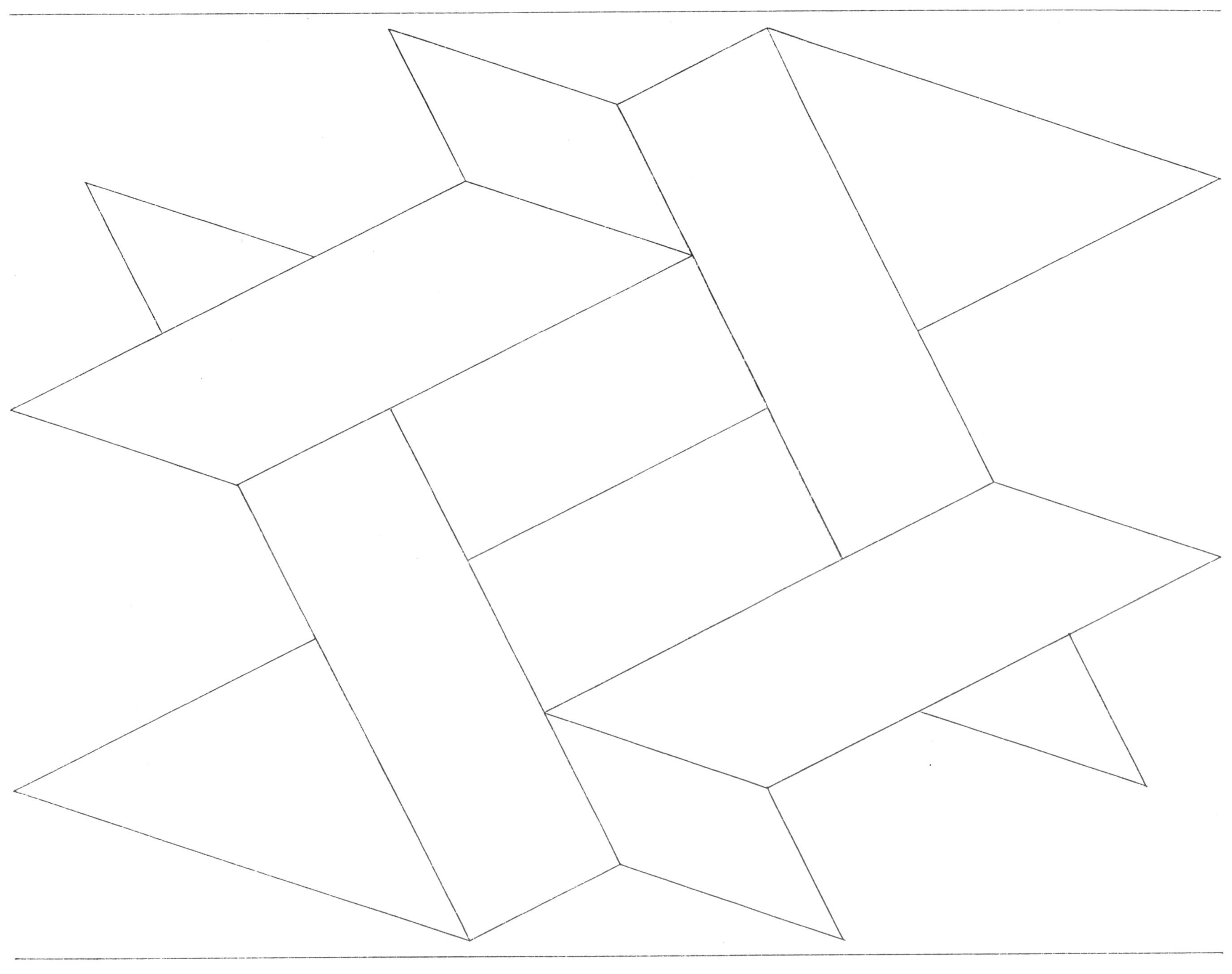

Je mehr

die Sonne scheint

desto mehr

Wasser verdunstet

Wolken erscheinen

und die Sonne

– scheint weniger

Je weniger

die Sonne scheint

desto weniger

Wasser verdunstet

Wolken werden weniger

und die Sonne

– scheint mehr

da capo

The more

the sun shines

the more

water evaporates

clouds appear

and the sun

– shines less

The less

the sun shines

the less

water evaporates

clouds diminish

aud the sun

– shines more

da capo

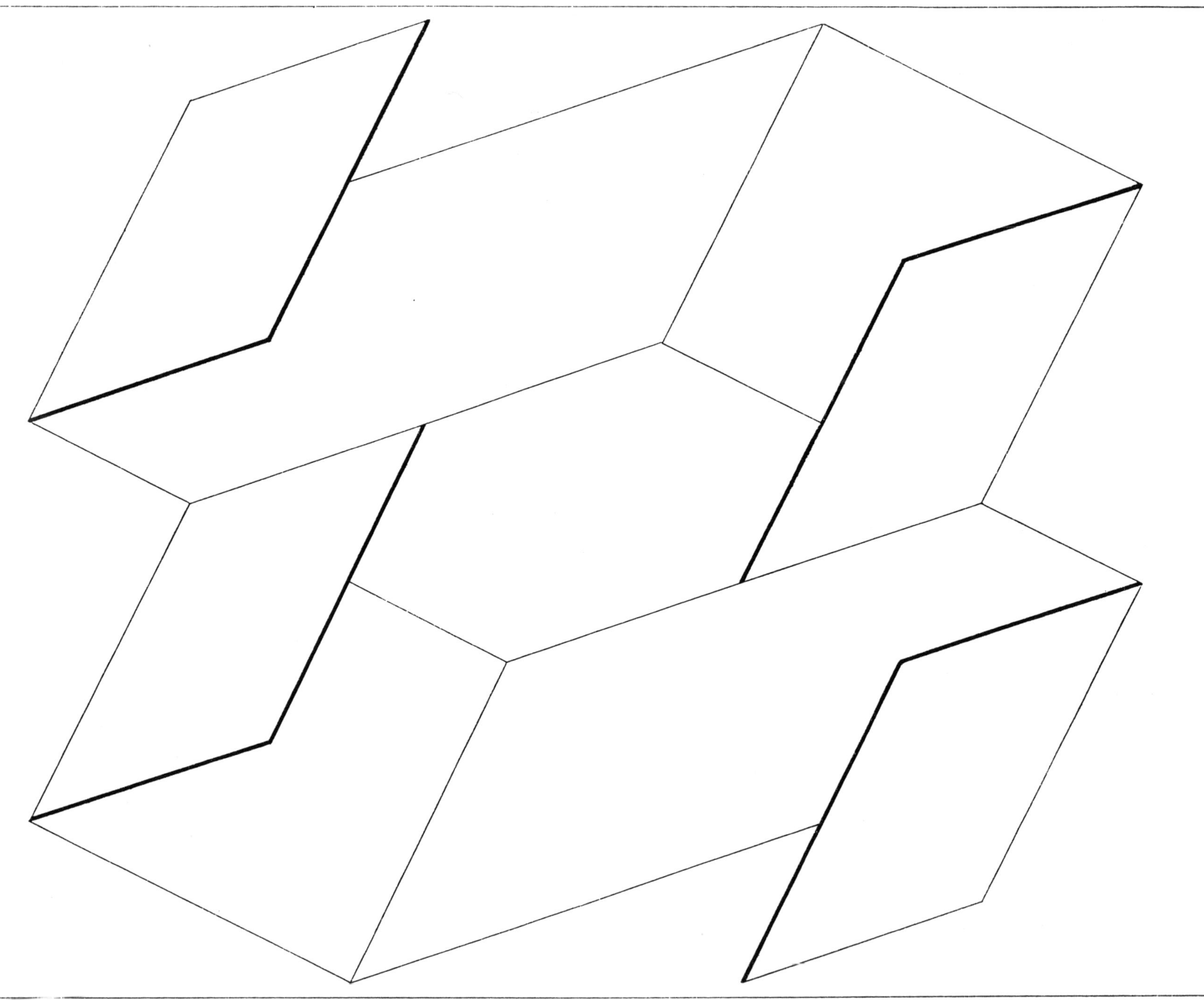

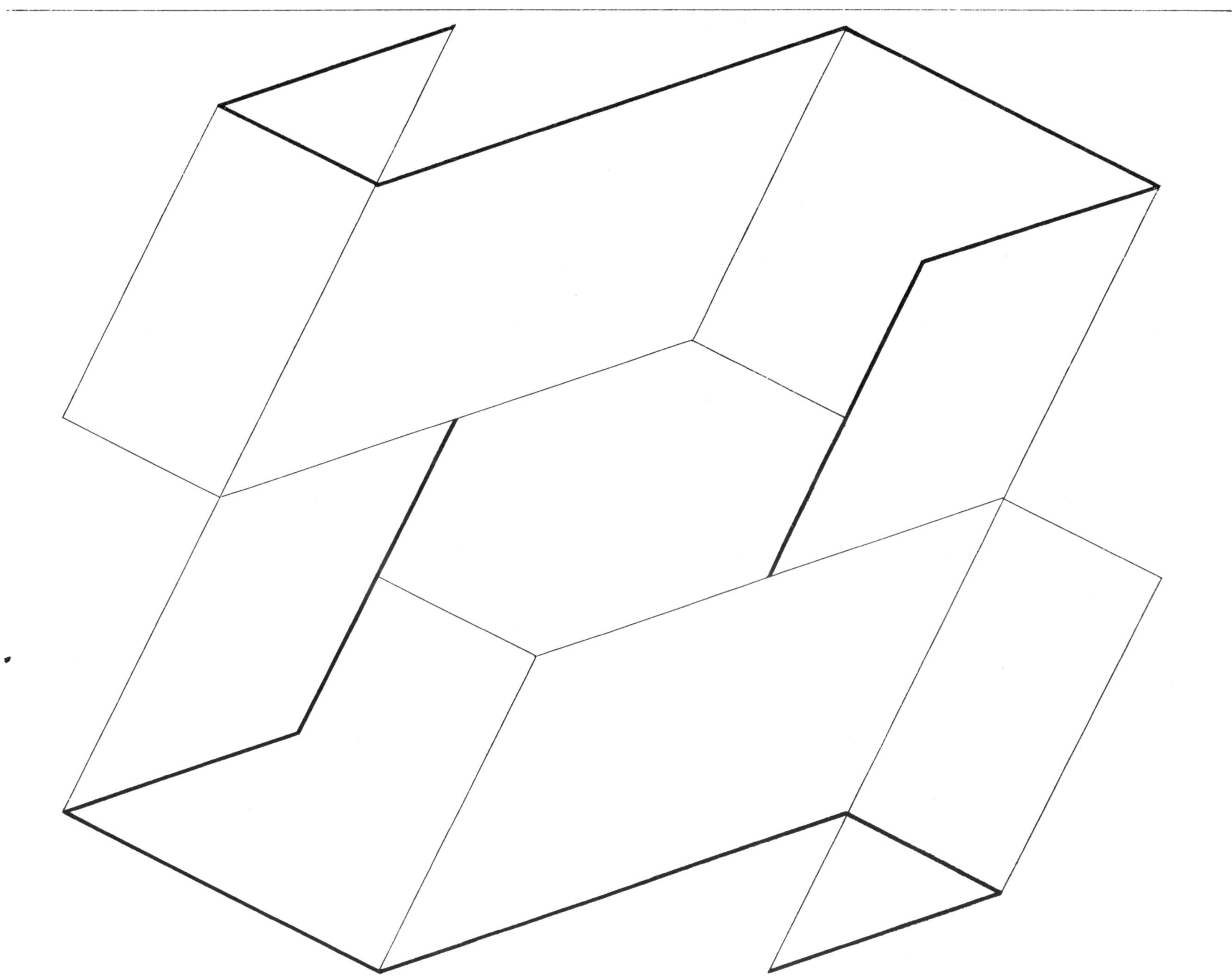

Man kämpft für –

was man selbst –

nicht hat

kämpft gegen die –

die ebenso –

wie wir

Lasst uns in Frieden

lieben was –

allen ist

zusammen geniessen

dass wir –

verschieden sind

One fights for –

what one doesn't have –

oneself

fights those –

who are –

like us

let's love in peace

that which belongs –

to all

and peacefully enjoy

our being –

unlike each other

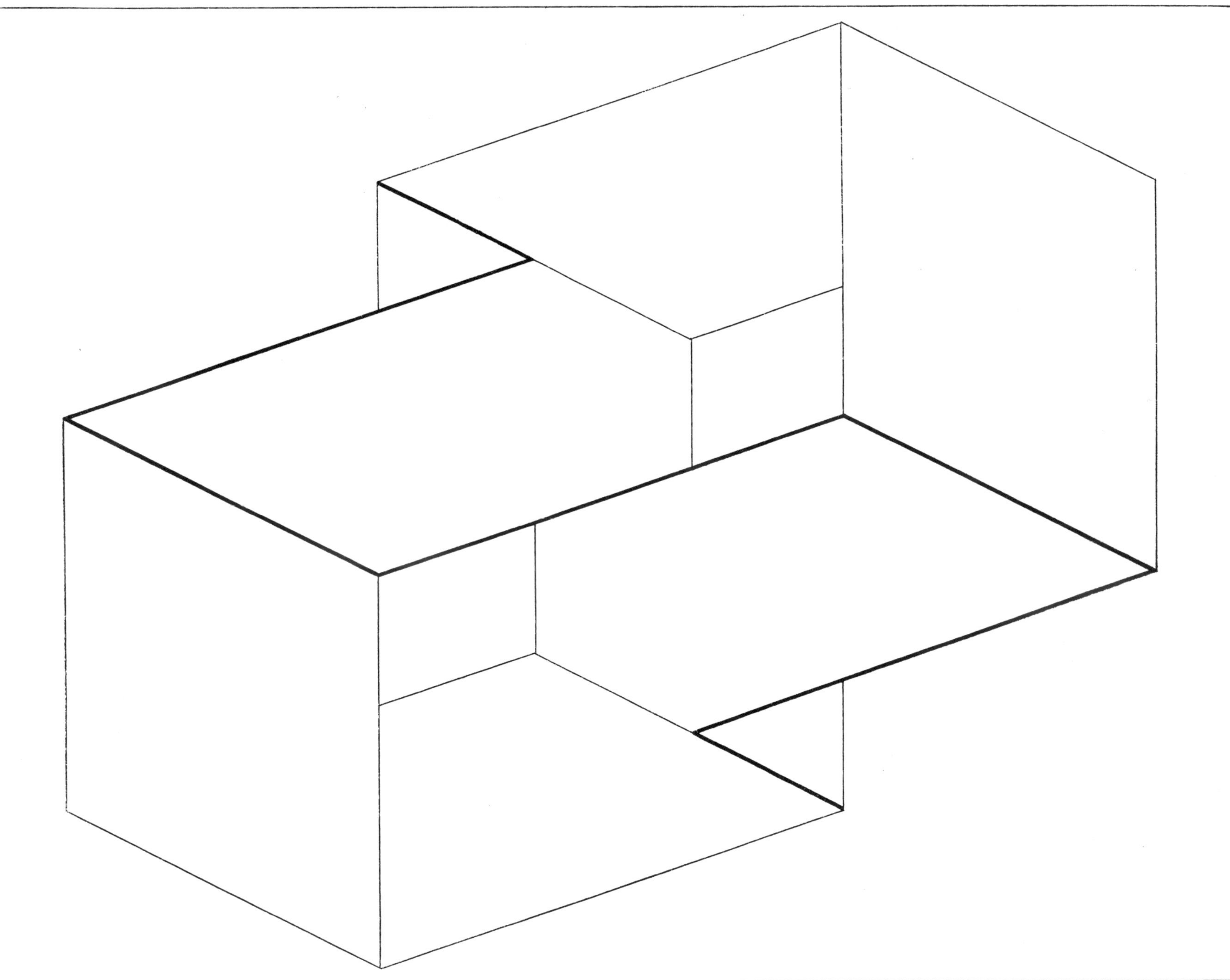

Keine Zeit ist – niemals

        niemals sowie überall

                überall ist immer

keine Zeit   *ist immer*

No time is – never

        never also everywhere

                everywhere is always

no time   *is always*

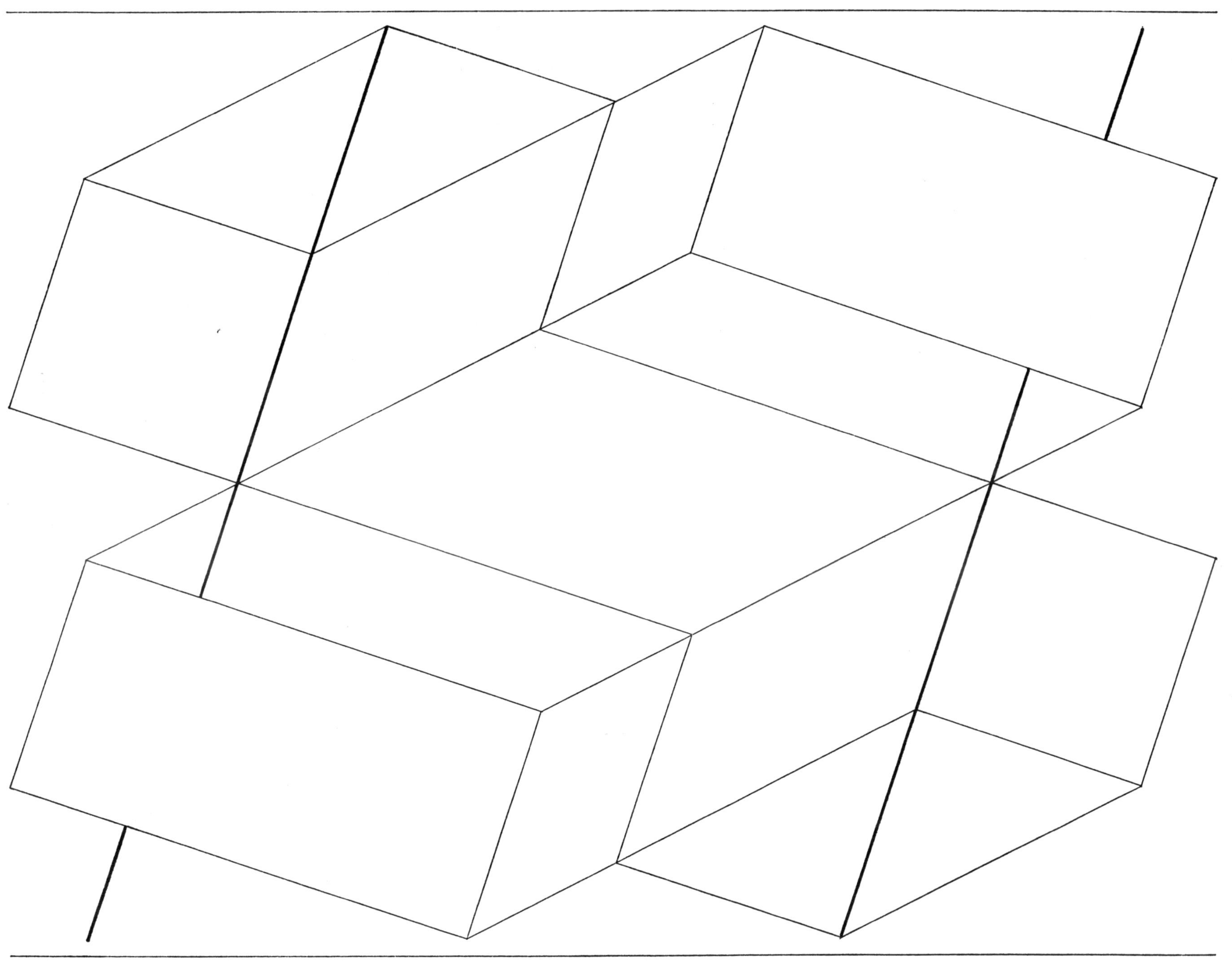

Keine Welt hat kein Theater

Niemand lebt für Nicht-erscheinen

Ohren sehen macht uns sprechen

Augen wissen macht uns zeigen

Sieh auch, dass Nicht-sagen spricht

Höre, dass auch Schwarz hat Farbe

Also muss der Schein nicht trügen

Jede Form hat Grund und Meinung

There is no world without a stage

and no one lives for not–appearing

Seeing of ears invites to speak

knowing of eyes invites to show

Notice also, silence sounds

listen to the voice of color

Semblance proves it can be truth

as every form has sense and meaning

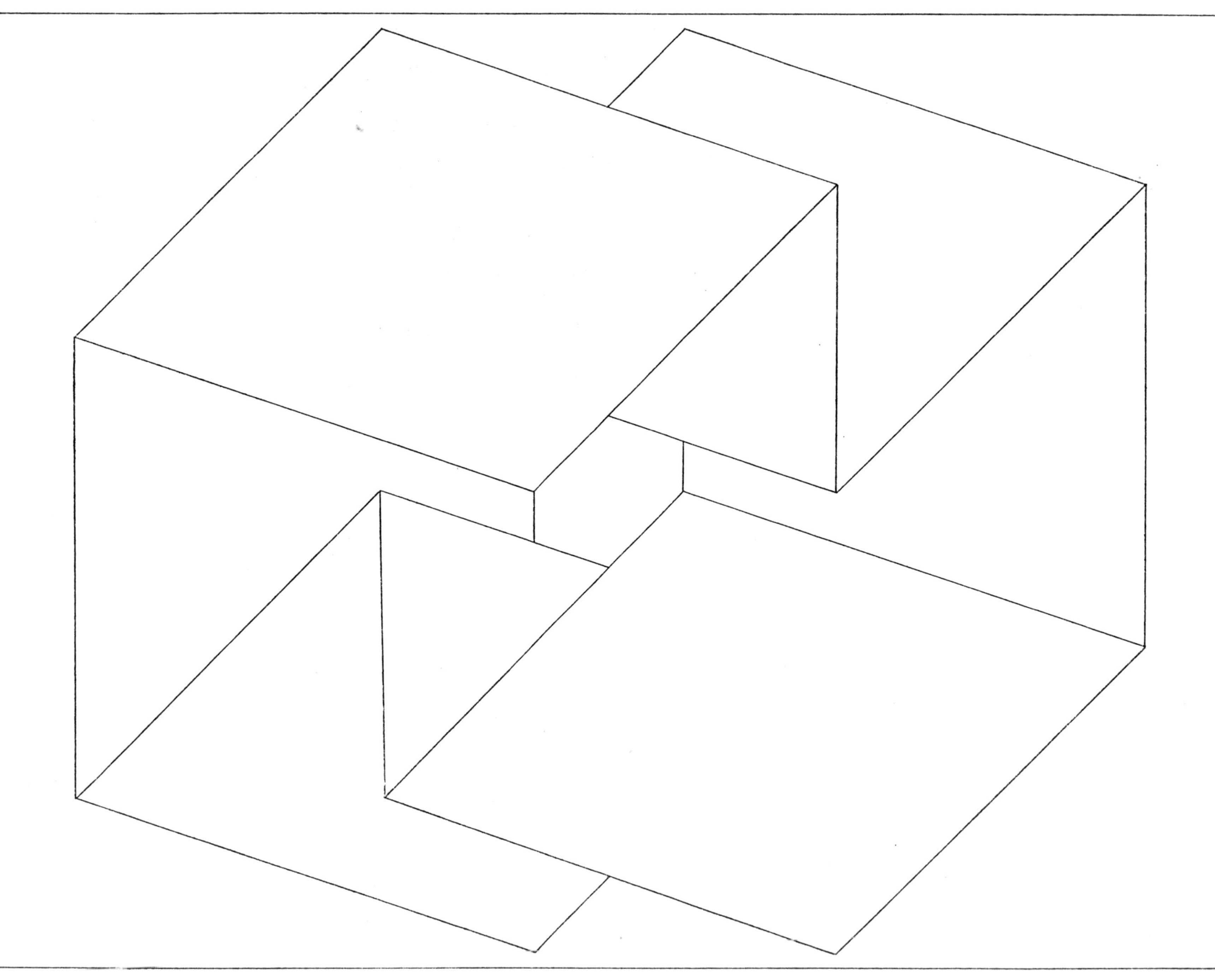

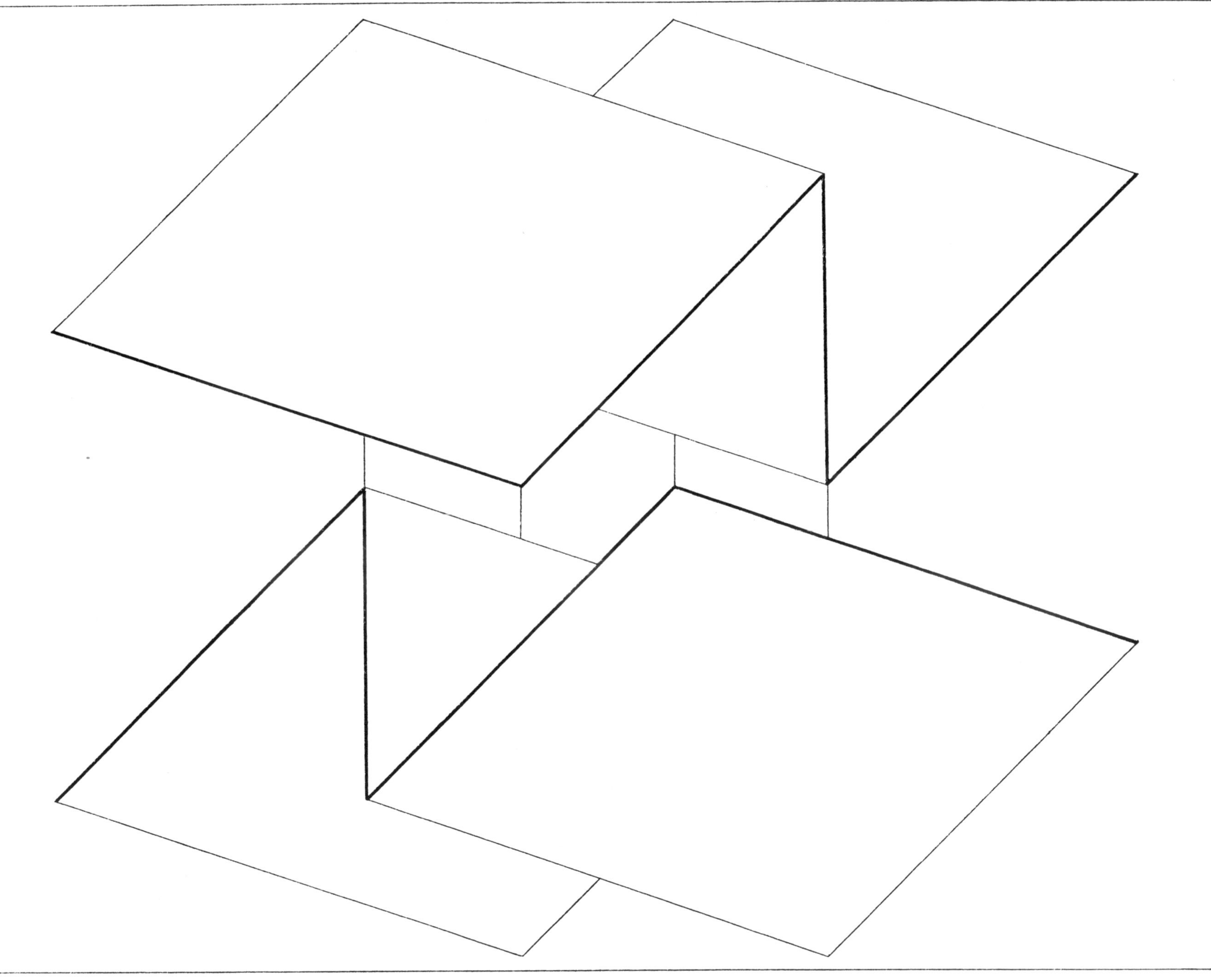

Beruhige dich

das meiste was geschieht

geschieht ohne dich

Calm down

what happens

happens mostly

without you

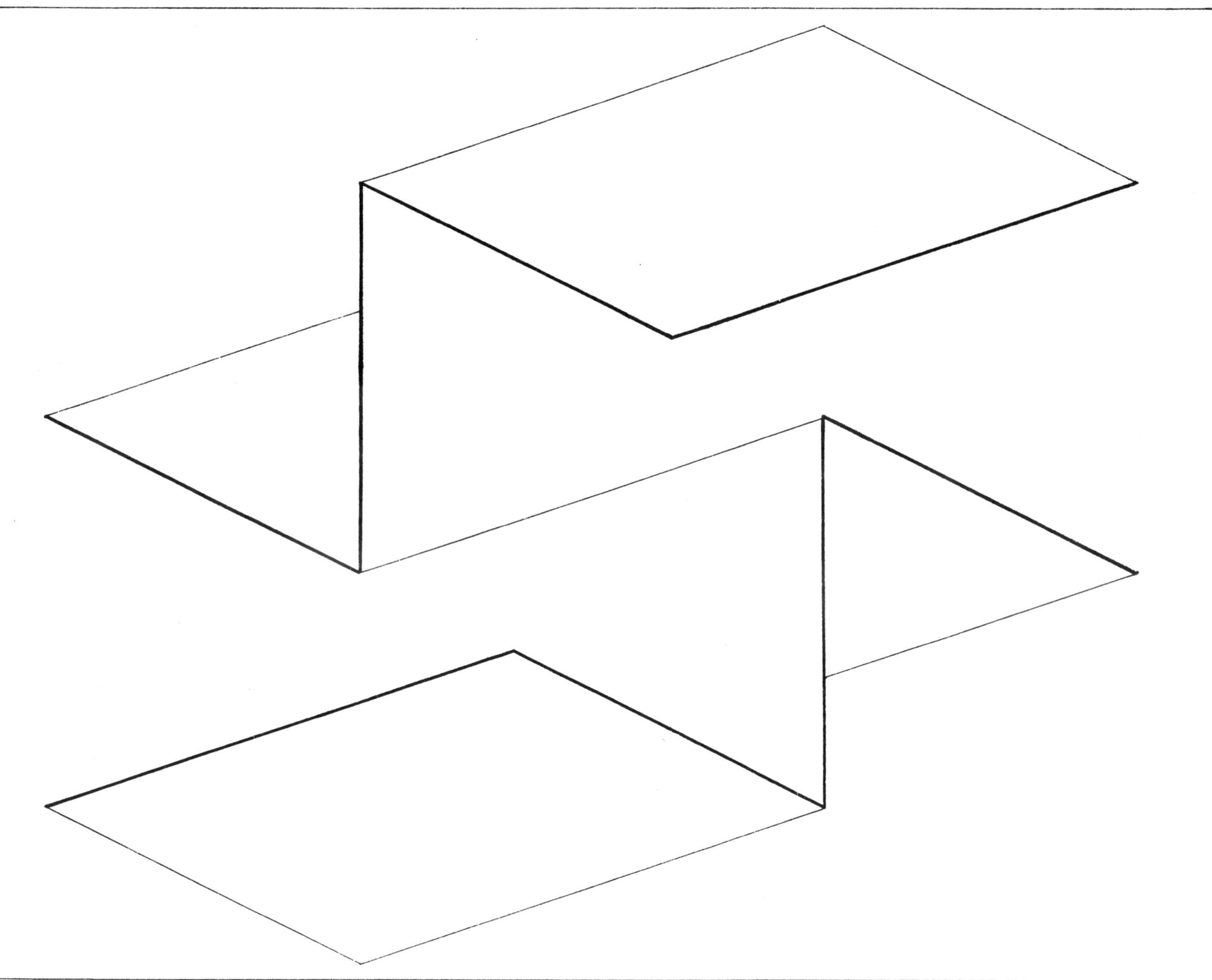

To distribute material possessions

is to divide them

to distribute spiritual possessions

is to multiply them

Verteilen sachlicher Güter

ist aufteilen – dividieren

Verteilen geistiger Güter

ist verbreiten – multiplizieren

Ergreifen erwirkt Besitz

Begreifen bewirkt Einsicht

Design and Sequence by Norman Ives